21 Glimpses of Mind

James Puterflam

BookLeaf Publishing

Presentation by *BookLeaf Publishing*

Web: www.bookleafpub.com

E-mail: info@bookleafpub.com

ISBN: 9789357612838

First edition 2022

DEDICATION

I would like to dedicate this book to all beings with sentience. May these poems come to benefit all who read them. Like the wind on the back of a boat's sails, may it serve as a force to propel you onwards in your journey through this event we call life.

ACKNOWLEDGEMENT

I want to say thank you to my dear friend Dr. Emma Ho who brought this writing challenge to my attention. Without her suggestion and motivation, '21 Glimpses of Mind' would not exist. I also want to thank my friend Cate Overend who has helped me with the rushed process of editing. Always insightful and informative with her amendments and suggestions. I want to thank all the inspiration for my writing. The many people, teachers, and experiences I have encountered throughout life so far. Most importantly I want to give a special thanks to my parents and spiritual teachers who motivate me and remind me of what is most important in this life.

PREFACE

The mind is described in different ways and referred to using different names depending upon one's cultural, philosophical, spiritual, or scientific education. Sometimes called 'mind', sometimes 'soul', 'spirit', 'consciousness', 'being' e.t.c. I have attempted as much as possible to describe the mind using lay terms which can be understood by people unfamiliar with other works discussing it. I feel it is important that the reader be aware of my biases and inspirations for they have shaped my use of language throughout. Primarily, as a scientist I always strive for clarity and honesty in communication and whilst poetry can be elusive, I have favoured the meaning on the majority of occasions. For this reason, at times the rhyming or melodic nature of my poems may be momentarily lost as to focus on its comprehension. When using the words, 'mind', 'soul', 'being', I am discussing it either in its most raw form or in its all encompassing manner. Whereas I occasionally use the terms, 'self' and 'ego', when discussing the more artificial, contrived or thought-generated one which we most frequently relate to on a regular basis.

Secondly, as a Buddhist, this is a key source of my experiences and inspiration when describing the appearance and nature of mind. I have not tried to describe anything I have absolutely no experience of, and I have avoided using Buddhist terms that readers would be unfamiliar with. This book is in no way an attempt to persuade or convert readers. It has been an honest attempt by myself as a human being, with the mind of a scientist and sceptic, to describe the way that 'mind', 'spirit', 'soul', 'being' e.t.c. appear and what its true nature is.

These poems are inspired by my own experience of the mind, which is little, as well as the writings of others, predominantly accomplished masters of Buddhism who dedicate their existence to understanding, experiencing and teaching the mind to others. Please be aware when reading that I have tried to use words to describe the appearance and function of the most elusive thing to exist (or not exist). I feel my attempt is no greater than someone trying to describe colours to a blind person or sounds to a deaf person. I further want to say that these poems are simply a combination of words which I have selected and that you will read and interpret. There may at times be some disconnect due to the differences in our minds. Do take your time to read, digest and reflect.

These poems will never replace genuine experience which is essential for anyone who is keen to develop certainty as to what the mind or being is and how it operates. If coming to understand your own mind is something that is meaningful to you, then I encourage you to keep going and I commend you for your efforts to do so. Many people are not interested in it, not one bit. I encourage you to pursue it by any means necessary, but do take care and be gentle with yourself in doing so. Examine all claims or assertions by others with a fine-toothed comb as carefully as you would if you were to purchase a diamond ring for the love of your life. Please also do so with what I have to say. Life is too short, and the questions are too many to delay it further. I hope these poems will benefit anyone who reads them, even if only to fill you with wonder and the enthusiasm to explore further. I want to apologise for any spelling or grammatical errors that are present throughout. The process of writing and editing over a 21-day period is a large task but one I was adamant to do. Nonetheless here it is. I offer you 21 Glimpses of Mind. This book is itself a reflection of my mind and one which will be interpreted by a reflection of your mind as well.

An Expedient Sermon on Time

Created by the past, the creator of the future,
The time is now, and forever always will be.

As yesterday meets tomorrow, the moon meets
the sun,
There is no dividing the stream of time.
How can one claim to be the same as they were
ten years ago,
One year ago, last week let alone yesterday?

Certainly, one cannot claim to be entirely the
same and unchanged,
Similarly, how can one deny that they are not the
product of developments since the beginning, or
beginningless, of it all.
Constantly time moves and so it acts to shape
all.

Forms, sounds, and constructs of the mind
continuously altered by the conditions of time,
Change, a universal law that affects all things
composed.

The whole is none other than the sum of the
parts,

and it is those parts that grow and decay,
Which are born and die, wax and wane,
Shaped and moulded without an end in sight.

On a day such as this, at a moment such as now,
one should stare directly down at the pool of
truth,
Present conscious, luminescent, and clear,
This present moment, the death of the past and
the birth of the future.

Clinging is fruitless, so are expectations,
Stay away from both.

Rest present in consciousness, the centre of time,
It holds onto nothing and remains nowhere,
unable to be pinpointed it is complete and
perfect,
Only is it seen, when time is let go.

With attention, free of ideals, one can watch it
effortlessly unfold,
The film most worth watching is the now of life.

Just a Moment Away

At any moment one may connect with the
simple essence,
As close as eyelashes yet challenging to see,
The more one exerts distractions, the more
difficult it grows,
Not captured or held, in every moment it flows,

Existent with all, unlimited, without bounds,
Immense as sky, holding all as space,
It cannot be claimed for one's own nor shared
like a gift,
The acquainted can point, yet only the finger-tip
is seen,

Unable to be purchased, sold, or exchanged,
Not built or made, present as the day,
Bright as the sun, watchful as the moon,
Inseparable as the ocean and her radiant waves,

All appearances are interdependent with its
child-like play,
There is nothing more pure, true or uncorrupted,
Richer and deeper than any fine wine,
The most precious and impressive of any
adornment,

Present always, since before and forever,
Ultimately essence-less, undisturbed as a mirror,
The instigator and witness of both joy and terror,
Lamp-like awareness, the charmer, the thriller.

Presence

It's ever present pure and undefined,
Evading all words, it's hard to find,
Despite its existence, nothing can confirm it,
The claims, the certainties, they're more or less
useless,

Like space it holds, but awareness is there,
Try to escape it, or give it a stare,
You'll see that it vanishes, like a shadow in the
sun,
Trying to chase it, you'll see how it runs,

Using it, we search for it, is this possible to do?
Like to see one's own face, or a moment yet
new,
The past is history, over and forgotten,
The future a mystery, a child yet begotten,

Accompanying all, with nothing to negate,
Present with action, it's alert and awake,
Beyond hold and beyond beck and call,
Soul or no soul, you'll find nothing at all,

The fruit of before and seed of after,
Obsessed with these two, the now's a disaster,

Yet placed in the moment, the only one to be,
Where the weather is fine, and space is free,

When crowded not, it's spacious as sky,
Whatever appears soon passes it by,
Concern it not with who, what, when and why,
Fixation free, in all directions let fly.

The Two, the One

A beginning not remembered,
A destination unsure,
Continuous without breaks,
Unending it snakes.

To heaven or to hell?
All doors it opens,
Angelic or demonic,
A poison or tonic,

The seer that's unseen,
A light without source,
A mirror with no dust,
Many years bare no rust,

Source of waves,
Mover of clouds,
Canvas for paints,
Sky over all,

The builder of hopes,
and dreamer of dreams,
The harbinger of doubts,
and architect of fears,

Awareness undisturbed,
Naked when unperturbed,
Authentic and natural,
Not nothing, not conceptual,

Looked for, it evades,
Like a dog pursues its tail,
It's too close to see,
Like trying to separate you and me,

Subject and object,
Try to find the gap,
Believing that there is one,
is the thickest of traps,

Luminosity unceasing,
Upon senses caught feasting,
Characteristics, without,
Yet existing, no doubt,

No shape, no colour,
No sound, no texture,
No smell, no taste,
No edge, no centre,

Days are never slowed,
Grass maintained must be mowed,
Loose holdings are wise,
Fixation is demise,

The ignitor of fires,
Also the extinguisher,
Cloud forming mires,
The interpreter of outsiders,

Clear and clarified,
Obstructed and smudged,
Confused and disoriented,
Or gentle steeper of love,

Inseparable from the present,
Appearing dual against 'things',
Good, bad, happy, sad,
It's there with all and anything.

The Sun, the Moon

What greets one in the morning,
And what guides one at night,
The dispeller of darkness,
And all actions the witness,

Hot glaring knowing,
Blurred hazy glowing,
Staring dazzled blind,
Burner of the eye,

Quiet and majestic,
Gentle and magnetic,
Calm and serene,
Seductive with gleam,

The beholder, the knowing,
The torch, the flowing,
The brightness, the clarity,
Ours has no disparity,

Onward it travels at the passing of life,
It leaves the corpse cleaner than cake on a knife,
Illuminating space and whatever appears,
Radiance spreading, free from all fears,

Attached to nothing, it has no hands to grab,
No eyes to see, nose to smell or tongue to taste,
Undeniably present, complete without waste,
No dawdling or haste, grasped at, it escapes,

No pollutant can taint it,
No additive can change it,
Pure, bright, and glowing,
Not shrinking, not growing,

Pervading out wide, to the edges of conception,
Free of these edges or centre of detection,
It's here now, it's here later,
No difference ever, the same taste is savoured.

The Garden

Green, vibrant, alive,
Then aged, decayed, demise,
Youthful, attractive and energised,
Then relinquished, skeletal, and dry,

A dwelling for life, and a place for death,
A source for joy, but also its theft,
Gentle support brings reward and success,
Neglect and avoidance and you'll receive much
less,

Soil, sun, wind, and rain,
The garden needs all plus toil to gain,
Scorched, it will overheat,
Drenched, it will drown at the feet,

Clean air riding gentle breeze,
And earth nutritious, toxin free,
A careful balance, it's a dance and an act,
Moments to let it be, and ones to enact,

The fruits reaped come from the seeds sown,
From tomato seeds, tomato plants grow,
Seeds of hate bare fire and rage,
Seeds of love breed contentment and space,

Desire brings tightness, hunger, and thirst,
Compassion blossoms in blissful bright bursts,
The garden-like mind requires attention and
care,
Deprive it decrepit, doomed if you dare,

Unpleasantness, foulness may help it contrive,
From undesirable waste, growth can derive,
A lotus pristine when emerged from the mud,
Beauty never left, just obscured by a smudge,

Radiant, captivating, dreamful, inspiring,
Sweat and tears makes the effort worthwhile,
The experience personal, the reward sweet,
Sweat on the hands, dirt on the feet,

The garden is all these things, so too the mind,
The grounds of all, nothing more one can find,
The spacious holder, the possessor of dual,
No 'thing' to fight, nothing to duel.

Busy Bees

Landing on one flower then off to the next,
All actions, feeding, toilet, and sex,
Plenty of colours passed on the way,
Is there anything which won't cause one to
sway,

Why the constant buzz of bees,
To many remains a mystery,
Perhaps to be occupied, constantly busy,
Appearing important, or simply ordinary?

The relentless nature of endless tasks,
An onslaught of doing never ever passed,
Goal after goal, an unending journey,
The road goes winding, ever onward turning,

The brewing, planning, ever conniving,
What's there more to do with all this surviving?
Hobbies, interests, work and worth,
How else to spend whatever time on earth?

Money, family, and health,
Accumulating forms of illusory wealth,
Chasing fame, it's all just games,
One day forgotten, the ever many names,

The achievements, investments crumbling all,
The moment they're built, one day to fall,
What's put together will one day come part,
Possessions now useless, a corpse can grasp
them not,

The indestructible, ineffable, onward to go,
Stuck it the now, to where we don't know,
It's not this, a thing, or any sort of construct,
The uncontrived self, for which no thing will
obstruct,

Yet always with games, we're eager to play,
Evading the unknown, passing up the day,
Day after day goes off on their way,
The contrived goes with them, only space
remains.

Ocean

Day after day we bob on away,
In some direction we flow,
Sometimes pulled with the current we go,
Going off where we don't know,

Deeply profound, mighty and proud,
Yet subtle and gentle with glee,
Unending, untamed, as far as eyes see,
Immense, playful, and free,

Dense at the centre, thin at the edge,
Stretching it kisses the land,
Lost at the end it laps on the sand,
Caught not when grasped by a hand,

Formation of waves a natural birth,
They rise and fall with a rapture,
They swirl, they whirl, free from capture,
To grow and dwindle, their nature,

A thought in the mind may arise a surprise,
Its presence seen without trace,
Maybe slow or quickening pace,
Round and round they chase,

Take just a drop, when then you stop?
Before the ocean's wealth is exhausted,
The sum of the many not just the one,
Its face changed by the sun,

Akin with us, but not longing lust?
Free from envy, desire, and thirst,
Always it wanders, the shoreline it skirts,
No hurt can cause it to burst,

Beyond control, to be embraced not owned,
Its formations appear as a dream,
Fed from rivers and child-like streams,
The ocean is not all it seems.

Gone Like the Wind

Left on its own the mind acts its own,
Left and right, always thoughts are blown,
Without a direction, intent, or plan,
Wandering off to sea or throughout all the land,

Far and wide if given the chance,
With anything encountered, as trance or a dance,
Alive and aware, uncontrived presence,
Yet when looked for, the source evanescent,

The past is where it was, the future where it will
be,
The present where it is, but always never seen,
Although there's no speck its existence is clear,
The celebrator of joy and trembler of fear,

Nor celebrator or trembler leave mark on its
tracks,
Free of characteristics there's nothing that it
lacks,
Fresh and spontaneous whenever it comes,
Wherever it goes, forever it runs.

The Cage

The container, the vessel,
Impenetrable metal,
Surrounding moments whenever,
Present wherever,

Unseen with eyes, a place of mind,
Existent without a speck to find,
Attempt at escape brings no avail,
Try to sail, the vessel will fail,

Every day, the same cell,
Sometimes heaven, sometimes hell,
Everyday chimes time's bell,
Death approaches, closer to fell,

In the morning when one prays,
Or in the evening as one lays,
Conjured up, the minds play,
Never stopping, night or day.

The Bird

Soaring, gliding way up high,
Upward, outward freely it flies,
Gliding gentle through the embrace of sky,
Into the blue, where the air is alive,

Pushed and pulled in the current of space,
Cutting and weaving with ease and with grace,
Free from grounding, shackle, or chain,
Loose is the mind, rewarding to train,

Spontaneous awareness striping the roof,
Long since bounded, clean is the hoof,
All clouds passed, falling back to their source,
Back to nothing, lighting to torch,

An understood mind moves a living art,
Yet treated as waste, like it's no more than a fart,
If it must be a fart, then let it out free,
Relaxed, released, in space let it be,

Free from worry, fear, and anxiety,
Charging clouds grey, provide them with
lightning,
Unleashing bolts across a sky burnt black,
Flashing at will, it echoes with cracks,

Nothing lacked on its feathery back,
This way or that, it's not important to track,
All that needs attention is the awareness of act,
The rest, impure, insidious, crap.

The Storyteller

The thoughts born at night,
Or conjured in the morning,
Those occurring in between,
Or with eyes shut, snoring,

Are they much different from a bedtime story?
Tales self-told, sadness or glory,
Unlimited, unhinged, anything can appear,
Vivid and clear, provocation of fear,

A story nonetheless, given life when they're
believed,
Emotions and feelings from memories retrieved,
Considered tangible or real, we have ourselves
deceived,
Anything at all can possibly be conceived,

A nightmare, a fairy-tale, a dream or a fable,
Sporadic, changing, crumbling, unstable,
Rolling and falling like water off a fall,
Tumbling and rumbling, each one, and all.

Gates of Hell

Through jagged gates we are pushed,
Where all rationality is shushed,
Within this place, a burning hotplate,
Fearsome fire, ferocious to taste,

What brings us here? Why's it not clear?
Distressed or responding to fear?
Defensive, protective, narrowly caged,
Mind seeping venomous rage.

Hate is not separate from mind,
Not a speck or place you will find,
Not recognized inwards so outward it flows,
Entangled ablaze is the soul,

The blame goes outer, when not witnessed inner,
Bewilderment swirls which may turn one a
sinner,
Thrown out, hatred's wings set soar,
Like a gale which blows a fire to roar,

Where did it come from? Where does it go?
Expression, uncontrolled, effortless unfold,
Witnesses claim a raucous red face,
But only the enraged face their faith,

It's all the mind I need not remind,
We walk through the gates but heed not the sign,
Why not turn around, flee molten hot ground,
Let it echo like a moment of sound.

Starved

Roaming endless in search of my fill,
Empty, but going, fuelled by sheer will,
Yearning and burning for a drop or a crumb,
That taste, that ecstasy, of craving undone,

Given a taste, the thirst ends not,
The stomach tied, twisted in knot,
Discomforted, seeing space on the plate,
Distorted, a burden, feeling of weight,

Satiety, illusory as approaching the horizon,
Hankering, pursuing, the throat becomes
tightened,
Possession, it's close, almost it's mine!
Yet a rental, temporary, finite with time,

Onto what's next, whatever catches the eye,
Maybe hips, some coin, a slice of cherry pie,
Chasing, wanting, ravenous for some,
Reached, acquired but the ending is numb,

Now that I'm done, surely, it's the end,
Wait just a moment, there's more at the bend,
Only once more and surely the end,
Puzzling, a riddle, the loop redescends

Round and round, there's no seeming end,
The results of ignorance, as baseless a trend,
Malevolence the result, the crazed will for more,
Something different, or maybe just more,

Screaming for help, without anyone to call,
Reaching the base of a bottomless hole,
Holding the sky or reaching for a star,
Conceptually grasping what you ultimately are,

Let it go, let it go then you'll have it all,
You'll be filled instantaneously, body and soul,
The hunger and thirst, satiated,
Released, unshackled, fully expatiated.

The Beast

In a world of its own, alone it roams,
Self-serving, self-centred, to few is it known,
In the darkness of night, it searches for light,
Unaware that itself, is the predator, the fight,

At the crack of dawn, it returns to its cave,
Avoiding the thing it needs to be saved,
Mad and crazed it howls away,
Alone in misery it wishes to stay,

All it dreams of is war,
Blood filling and flooding the floor,
Bones grizzled and gnawed,
Sharp as razors, its claws,

Reactive to all, it's wild untamed,
By whatever appears its easily swayed,
Without reason, discipline or peace,
Vicious and wild toward all without cease,

All which arises, confronts it a threat,
On guard, alert, for a challenge to be met,
Defending its name, protecting its place,
Unwilling to glare its truth in the face,

Fuelled by anger and bitterness,
It's seduced by the ways of wickedness,
Reasoning impossible, sick to the core,
Locked and shut it closes the door.

Moving

Why the talk of heaven and hell,
If you want to see them, then do so in your cell,
Your cell or mind will take you there,
Anywhere and everywhere, wherever you dare,

All you need is a moment, all you need is a
push,
A catalyst, a charge, a sudden surprise or
ambush,
A trigger, a memory, laughter, a scream,
All in a moment, from real to a dream,

From dream to real, all is not what it seems,
Like the light we see, travelling as beams,
It's never the same, like the burning of a flame,
Connected, continuous like carriage and train,

Smoothed and coalesced, experience is made,
All stuck together, growing only to fade,
Put together it's no more than a meal,
The resources, the effort, for a temporary fill,

Now you are happy, elated, and proud,
Next moment sad, depression enshrouds,

Suddenly noise, clashing rambunctious and loud,
Soon passes winds on quite hill mounds,

Forwards, onwards the direction of now,
Boring or exciting does it really matter how?
All is changing, always rearranging,
Fixate on anything it'll be your displacing.

The Watcher

As the riddle goes-

Does the fallen tree make a sound,
Even if there's no one around,
Does anything occur if there is no witness?
How can anything known not be seen?

The watcher, the seer, the subject,
If an object is without one, then is it no less
reject?
For the eyes, ears, and senses elect,
What's occurred and now been detect,

A magnificent painting without any viewers,
Beauty and looks without admirers,
Pain and suffering without an endurer,
Seed, sun, and rain but not any manure,

An orchestra singing music of bliss,
But what if without ears to listen?
A chef cultivates a delightful dish,
But what if without tongue to taste?

A fresh flowers fragrance flowing fruitfully free,
But with if without a nose to smell,

The king governs to better the land,
But what if without subject to better,

The physician heals the ill with her skill,
But what if without those who are sick,
The teacher bestows knowledge to the dumb,
But what if without students in class,

The dream, the wish, the thought,
Appearing as they are seen,
The object dependent on subject,
Without subject what have they been?

Without subject there is nothing worthy
speaking of,
So, the ego will say,
The show is separate from the audience,
So, the ego insists,

This happening, I watching,
So, the ego will play,
This body, this mind,
So, the ego will claim.

Pointing Out

Here and now is the opportunity,
Nonetheless it is one that goes begging,
Here is the moment, past and futures unity,
Nonetheless when you look, the meeting isn't
seen,

Are these words really separate from the one I
call you?
They might appear external, yet they depend on
you,
In this experience of you, reading words,
You, reading, words, needed together are these
few,

What are you, other than body, mind and name?
What is a body but bones, blood, and brain,
What is a mind but thoughts, feelings, and
memories,
How about the name we spend much time
protecting?

Reading is an act played out by eye,
Disabled by the dark, rendered by the light,
Words is just an assembly of letter and sound,
w-o-r-d makes word possible,

There's really no end, you can refine it
furthermore,
Take the mine now, have a look what it's for,
The essence of appearances evades mind's eye,
No one has seen a face, seeing nothing is right,

Its shape obscured complete,
A colour on no spectrum,
A size not big nor small,
A location not here nor there,

Some may call it boring or supremely
unexciting,
Others fear the truth, dreadful and frightening,
The supreme see it clear, despite its plain sight
hiding,
In space unobstructed, effortless abiding.

Immortal

The desire of immortality is naturally
accomplished,
Yet not in the way that Hollywood worships,
Unchanging is minds nature, soul, or essence,
The names are endless and so to its expression,

The basis, the ultimate, beyond conception,
Yet I'll attempt to explain, what I've heard
mentioned,
We spend our lifetimes accumulating and
chasing,
Wealth, beauty, fame, friends, and family,

Recognized not enough, where all this must go,
When the time calls, we'll leave this corpse
below,
All the many constructs, physical or mental,
Possessed or pursued, nothing more than
eventful,

Outlasting all that's made is what we don't see,
What we cannot find, imprisoned instead of free,
The expanse, alive space, beyond word or
thought,

Unchanged by what appears, like reflections never caught,

The construct of self, the trickiest of the lot,
Thoughts, feelings, memories, this animate corpse,
Yet all these things change, whilst awareness ends not,
From evening to morning, without pause or a stop,

All that's constructed must change, evolve, or rot,
The unconstructed and unseen, assigned this rule they are not,
Enjoy the immortality unchanging, unending non-stop,
Perfect and pristine, perceived it is not.

Dancing with Appearances

Real or imagined both reside within the mind.
Inside or outside is there any essence you can
find?
Like a bubble or a rainbow, present yet unstable.
An illusion conjured existent, yet essentially
unreal.

Not solid or concrete, fluid and dynamic.
All appears a slight of truth, like a magician's
trick.
Slick and slimy, it slips conceptual grasp.
Vibrant, existing, every moment is its last.

Inner and outer, are they the same or different?
Ultimately indistinguishable like day and night's
collision.
No interruption, they occur blurred and blended.
No separation, like the sky and the horizon.

The feelings of joy, sadness, and hurt,
Disgust and desire, anger, or surprise,
None have permanence and none have a face,
They exist and act in no particular place,

Like a breeze upon the face on a windy day,

Present then gone, present then gone again,
Give no great importance to experiential play,
Never-ending, ever rolling, as day follows day,

Inescapable, impermanent, appearing as it likes,
Hold it or reject it, see what that is like,
Burning and uncomfortable, like a flame within
the chest,
"Go away, I don't want you" – the habitual way
to act,

With calm upon the mind, answers you will find,
Rest in the moment, free of wanting to cry,
Let it all drop and see what calls attention,
Maintain awareness yet rest without intention,

Look and watch like you're stuck within a cell,
Calmly abiding, witness heaven-hell,
Whatever appears, may stoke fires of desire,
Except for the unveil there's nothing further to
admire,

Action brought them here, but from where did
they come and where do they go?
They appeared and affected me, but they've
nothing else to show?
They were so real, like a vibrant rainbow,
Cling not to this conception but through action
let it show.

For whatever does appear one should learn to let
it go,
Most important is the response, from the mind
that truly knows,
One who acts without acting will be calm and
unperturbed,
Or else it's just words, a captivating magic show.

The Beginning, the End

From what moment did it begin, and where is its
end,
A question for the clairvoyant or those who
condescend,
The normal way to feel is that surely there is
one,
Look at all else and the course that they run…

The dawn of day and the falling of night,
When is one born and the other taken flight,
When the sun rises up, or falls down from the
sky,
When does that occur, at what point do they die?

Before it's even seen, light grows and spreads,
The reverse when it departs, a dense dark
descends,
The appearance of the bright spot, an arbitrary
means,
An occurrence, a name, a constant moving thing,

Not still for one moment, transitioning through
space,
Not so different from the mind in a race,
Moving metal rust on a regular basis,

Composition free from any state of stasis,

The organic, the compounded, changing,
rearranging,
Appearing as forms and shapes but truly all are
empty,
No not nothing, but dependent arising,
Dependent on actions, on others, and
surroundings,

The self is the body, its parts, and organs,
The self is the mind, its thoughts, memories, and
emotions,
The self is the name, the sound, associations,
and pride,
The self is compounded, a shape with many
sides,

Without apparent beginning it develops as we
play,
Without a distinguishable end it will diminishes
when we lay,
It is always the beginning, and it is always the
end,
The past and the future, now do they depend.

www.ingramcontent.com/pod-product-compliance
Lightning Source LLC
LaVergne TN
LVHW021252200726

843509LV00012B/1645